Date Due

MOUNTAINS

by DELIA GOETZ

Illustrated by
Louis Darling

William Morrow & Co. New York, 1962

The author wishes to thank Katheryne Thomas
Whittemore, Professor of Geography, State University College at Buffalo, Buffalo, N. Y., for checking
the manuscript.

CONTENTS

Mountains are the highest lands on the face of the earth. They are also among the least known.

Long ago primitive peoples feared them. They believed that witches, wizards, dragons, giants, and other fearsome creatures had their homes in the high places. And when they were forced to travel through the mountains, many people were carried blindfolded to shut out the sight of them.

Throughout history some people have believed that mountains were sacred places, because the gods lived there. Each year long lines of pilgrims climbed the sacred mountains to pray before the shrines of their gods. Even today many people look at the heights with awe. The Mexican peasant stands with hat in hand to gaze at the peak of Popocatepetl. And each year people who still honor ancient gods climb the mountains sacred to them in Japan, Korea, and Burma.

Others avoided the sacred mountains, be-

cause they feared that the presence of human beings would disturb and anger the gods. Nepalese guides are still afraid to climb certain mountains for that reason.

Early traders and travelers had other motives for bypassing the mountains if possible. Travel was difficult over unmarked routes on rugged heights, which were lashed by harsh winds and frequent storms. Travelers had to look for lower passes, or take roundabout ways to get across. Usually they took guards on the trips too, for the lonely heights were often the haunts of bandits, who preyed on travelers.

Inca and llama

But despite ancient fears and beliefs and the hardship of life, people do live in some parts of most mountains. Some of them sought refuge there to escape the tyranny of other tribes or nations. The Inca people, living in the Andes of Peru, retreated even higher into the mountains to escape the Spanish conquerors. Today the Berber tribes move higher and higher into the Atlas Mountains in Africa, so they can avoid their enemies.

Some people, like the early pioneers in the United States, settled in the mountains by accident. They set out for lands beyond the mountains, but stayed in the highlands, because they liked the life there. Others suffered illnesses or other bad luck, and got no farther.

And today, as in ancient times, many religious people live alone in the mountains to meditate and pray. In Tibet holy men turn their prayer wheels, as they have for centuries. And in mountains around the world other religious men live in monasteries.

Whatever people have felt about them and wherever they have lived, mountains have affected their lives in some way.

holy man
of Tibet

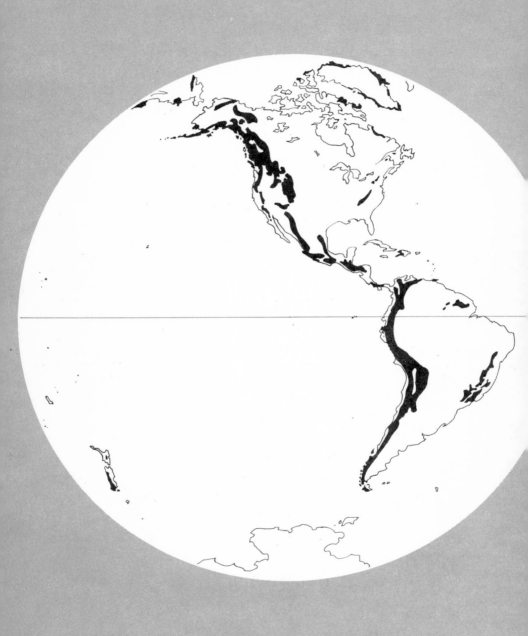

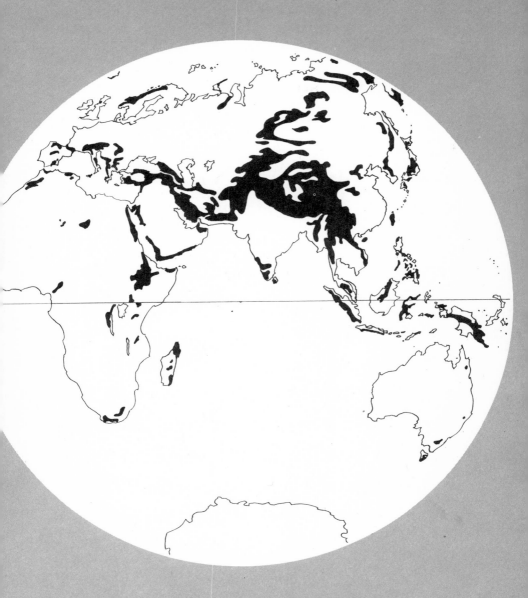

MOUNTAINS OF THE WORLD

Look at the map and you will see that every continent has mountains. On some continents they are more continuous or more numerous than on others. High mountains sprawl over much of Asia. Australia, on the other hand, has only a small mountainous section. These high lands amount to about ten per cent of the earth's exposed surface. And great mountain ranges that rise from the floor of the sea may be even more extensive than those on land.

Among the great mountains of the world are those that ring the Pacific Ocean, broken here and there by valleys, plains, and high plateaus and interrupted by oceans and seas. They begin in Antarctica, and are found again in South America, where the Andes Mountains form a long and unbroken part of the ring. From the Strait of Magellan to the Caribbean Sea, the

Patagonian
mountains

Andes make a continuous wall. The mountains
of Central America, Mexico's Sierra Madres,
the Coast Ranges, the Cascades, the Sierra
Nevada, and the Coast Mountains of Alaska
and British Columbia form more of the ring.
Then it curves around to the western side of
the Pacific, extending through the Aleutians,
Japan, and other islands and rounding out the
circle again in Antarctica.

Swiss
Alps

The greatest mountainous area of the world lies in Asia. It includes such lofty ranges as the Himalayas, the Hindu Kush, the Caucasus, and others. The high mountains of southern Europe include the Alps, the Carpathians, the Pyrenees, and other mountains of Spain.

In addition to these massive ranges, mountains are scattered throughout the world—in Africa, in the eastern parts of North America and South America, in the islands of the Caribbean and the Pacific, and in northern Europe.

Bora-Bora Island
Pacific

Some, like the Appalachian Highlands of the United States, are old mountains that were formed hundreds of millions of years ago. Through the years their peaks have been worn down, their slopes have become more

Appalachian Mountains

gentle, and their valleys have broadened.

The sharp peaks and steep slopes of mountains like the Rockies and the Himalayas show that they are young mountains. But a young mountain may be millions of years old.

HOW MOUNTAINS ARE FORMED

A mountain is formed by forces within the earth, which cause its crust to take different shapes. In some places, strain and pressure push it into large folds, much as a rug wrinkles when the ends are pushed toward the center. Some folds are high, with narrow spaces between them. Others are wide, with broad spaces between. Under great pressure some of the folds bend over across others. Sometimes they give way and the rocks crack.

fold

fault

Mountains are also formed in other ways. Sometimes great cracks split far down and around a mass of rock. The rock pushes up, away from the cracks, like a huge block raised above the land around it. Unequal pressure underneath pushes one side of the block higher than the other and forms a steep slope.

Sometimes molten rocks, forced upward with tremendous pressure, form domes, like huge blisters, under the earth's crust. There they harden. In time, the softer rock lying above them wears away, leaving the domes exposed high above their surroundings.

Often hot lava forces itself against the earth's crust and strikes a weak spot. The crust gives way, and then the hot lava flows out and around the opening, cools, and becomes solid. This happens again and again, building higher and higher, to form a mountain. Other times lava is forced from a pipelike opening, and builds a high cone.

Many mountains are formed by combinations of these different forces.

As mountains are formed by action under

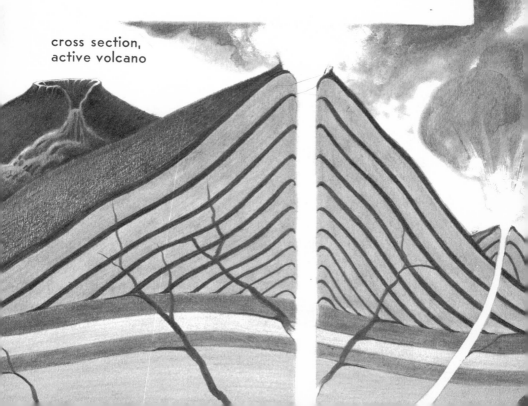

cross section,
active volcano

the earth's crust, they are also shaped by action from the outside. Rapid changes in temperature, from the heat of day to the cold of night, cause rocks to crack. Bits of rock and sand, blown against sharp peaks, smooth them and wear away soft rock. Rain freezes in cracks, widens them, and loosens pieces of rock. Flowing water carries away the loosened rocks and carves gullies and gorges into the mountainside. Masses of moving ice and snow scoop soil off the slopes and gouge valleys.

And so, although mountains may seem permanent, they are always changing, wearing down bit by bit, while new ones are being built. Old mountains, long since worn down, may rise again, and form highlands just as they did before. But these changes occur so slowly that they can scarcely be noticed in the lifetime of one person.

Rocky Mountains

The different ways in which mountains are formed, as well as their different locations, give them endless variety. No two ranges are exactly alike. The Andes differ from the Alps. The Great Smokies are different from the Rocky Mountains. Mount Kilimanjaro in Africa differs from Mount Everest in Asia, Acon-cagua in Argentina, or Mount McKinley in Alaska.

But all mountains are alike in a few certain ways. All mountains rise high above their surroundings. Their summits are smaller than their bases, and usually the slopes are steep.

Great Smokies

MOUNTAIN CLIMATES

Mountains are alike in other ways. They act as barriers to air and rain, and they affect temperature. For this reason mountain regions are said to have their own climate.

Sometimes they are rainier than the nearby lowlands. When moisture-bearing winds blow toward mountains, they are forced upward. The air cools as it rises. If it cools enough, the moisture in the air condenses, and clouds, rain, or snow result. Often the windward sides of mountains receive more rain than the leeward, or opposite, sides, where winds grow warmer as they descend the slopes.

Land on the leeward side of the mountains may also be very dry in contrast to the land on the rainy windward side. Most winds that blow over mountainous Hawaii are from the east and bear moisture from the Pacific Ocean. This falls as rain on the eastern slopes, but west of the mountains the land is dry.

rain shadow

cooler

warm, tropical

Mountain climates often differ in temperature as well as in rainfall. Moving up a mountain, one finds the air colder as one goes higher. This change in temperature accounts for another characteristic of mountain slopes. Vegetation that grows in widely separated zones in the lowlands may grow on the same

snow line

tree line

mountain. This change in vegetation is seen best on high mountain slopes of the tropics, where lands at the base are hot. At the foot of a mountain slope of Ecuador one may find fields of sugar cane and vast plantations of bananas. Farther up the mountainside, where it is cooler, grains grow, vegetables are firm and crisp, and there are trees. Still farther up, where it is cold, trees are small and scarce; farms become smaller and smaller until they are tiny patches, clinging to the mountainside; and the coarse grass grows in scattered tufts. The days are cold, and winds lash the heights.

TRANSPORTATION

Mountains act as great barriers across the earth and have an important effect on the way countries develop and how people live. In many places they divide a country into sections, each like a little world of its own, with no travel or communication between them. Language and customs may differ as much on each side as if they were separate countries. Massive mountains also form walls between nations in many parts of the world. Airplanes that crisscross the world can soar over their rugged heights, but in many places the only other way to travel is to go by foot over the steep, rocky trails.

Centuries ago the Inca people in the high

Inca road, bridge, and post-runner

Andes linked corners of their vast mountain
empire with roads, and spanned deep canyons
with bridges. But such roads were the excep-
tion, and when the Incas were conquered, the
roads were not kept up.

Modern engineers and road builders have now come along and built railroads in the mountains. At enormous cost in money and labor they built Peru's Central Railway, the highest standard-gauge railway in the world. Sixty-five tunnels were bored and eleven switchbacks were used to reach the highest point, almost three miles above sea level.

Engineers in the United States also faced many problems in building railroads in the mountains. A six-mile-long tunnel connects Denver with the western side of the Rocky Mountains, and another tunnel, eight miles long, runs under the Cascade Mountains. In all, the railroads use about 1400 tunnels to travel through our mountains.

But many mountainous countries have little or no railroad transportation. Honduras has no railroad to link its capital with the rest of the country. In Nepal's highlands travel is still mostly along well-worn footpaths.

Building highways through mountains is also difficult and expensive, but progress is slowly being made, and more roads are connecting isolated places with the rest of the world. Highways connect the cities of the Andes with the lowlands. And in the United States new roads have helped people find new vacation lands in the mountains. People in the mountains have found fresh markets for their products in this way. They have also benefited from roads in other respects. Over them come doctors, nurses, and teachers, who are helping the mountain people to live and work more comfortably.

WEALTH FROM THE MOUNTAINS

More roads and railroads will help to bring out the minerals locked in the mountains, for these rugged barriers in the path of people's movement are also the source of products for their use. Mining is one of the chief industries in many mountainous lands. As the mountains were slowly building, forces deep within the earth pushed great masses of lava

molten
rock (lava)

layers of
solid rock

upward. Some of the lava contained minerals, which were deposited in cracks in the surrounding rocks. Many of these are such valuable minerals as gold, silver, uranium, and precious stones of all kinds. But other minerals from mountain mines are no less valuable in our lives, for they are contained in things we use daily, such as coal, copper, iron, magnesium, tin and a long list of others.

Salt is also mined in many mountains. Famous among these mines are those in Colombia, South America, which has more than fifty miles of salt in its mountains. And the salt mines of Austria's Salzberg Mountain have been worked for more than forty centuries.

coal mine

Another valuable resource of some mountains is the forests that cover their slopes. A great many of the world's timber reserves are in these areas. Giant redwoods grow on the moist slopes of California's Coast Ranges. Tall Douglas firs, spruce, hemlock, and many other trees grow in the mountainous sections of the United States.

Forests also cover the slopes in other countries. Many different trees grow on the lofty

Himalayas, but most famous are the dense forests of cedar. In China and Japan, as well as other parts of Asia, in Europe and the Americas, forests furnish wood for lumber, paper, and many additional articles.

These forests on the mountains are also useful in a different way. Roots and fallen leaves hold the water from rain and melting snow and ice, and keep it from rushing down the slopes and flooding the lands below. The strong roots of trees and plants hold back the soil and prevent it from being washed down the slopes.

Water from mountain snow is used to irrigate farm lands. Often lands that are dry because of mountains are irrigated from mountain streams.

Mountain streams are also important sources of electric power. Water from the highlands of Italy, Norway, and Switzerland is converted into water power and widely used in the lowlands. Water power is one of Nepal's greatest resources. As the world's supplies of coal and other fuel grow scarcer, water power will become even more important.

Mountainous land is usually poor for farming. The soil is often thin and rocky. Slopes are too steep and farms too small for the farmer to use machinery, so all work must be done by hand. But in countries with dense populations or with little level land, people do farm the mountains. Their tiny farms cover the steep slopes like a patchwork quilt made of green grass, dark soil, and yellow grain.

On some mountain slopes farmers have built terraces to make more space for crops. The terrace walls are made of stone and they are built high to hold the soil brought up from below. Each year more soil is added to replace that which has been washed away.

Not all mountains are difficult places for growing crops. The sunny slopes are preferred to lower lands for vineyards and for other fruits that need long hours of sunshine.

In countries with little level land for growing crops, every bit of grass that grows must be used. Men with spiked shoes, to keep them from slipping down the precipice, cut the clumps of grass that grow between the rocks.

Bringing the hay down the mountainside can be just as dangerous as cutting it. Usually the men bring huge loads on their backs down the rocky paths. Sometimes it is stored on the mountain, and brought down on sleds in the winter. That, too, is often a dangerous trip.

In the United States, where farm land is not scarce, high mountains are used mostly for grazing animals. In the Southwest, when the grass in the valleys is short and brown, herders drive long lines of animals to mountain pastures to spend the summer.

In countries like Norway and Switzerland, taking the cattle to the mountain pastures is a time for holiday. Even the townspeople shut up shop and join the procession up the mountainside. And after long, dark days in the stables, the animals seem glad to be out in the sunlight.

MEN OF THE MOUNTAINS

Many scientists have work that takes them to the mountains. Often they spend months, even years, in some of the loneliest spots on earth. Some of them are men who search the high places for plants and animals that can now be found only in the mountains. Lands lower down have been cultivated, and plants that once grew wild have been uprooted and lost. Some plants, which grew first in the mountains, have been brought to lower lands to grow. It was in a rocky, bare corner of a Korean highland that a plant hunter found the regal lily. And the blue alfalfa, now a valuable food in cattle-raising countries, was brought from a far-northern corner of Asia.

Great herds of animals that roamed the lower lands have been killed by hunters, and the few that escaped have fled high into the

mountain goat

bighorn sheep

mountains. Sheep and many types of deer live only on the heights. Men have followed treacherous trails to find rare animals for zoos.

ibex

Other men study the heavens and the stars from mountains. In great domed observatories on Mount Palomar and Mount Wilson in California and on Mont Blanc in Switzerland, men sit before powerful telescopes to study the constellations.

And here and there, in some of the highest, least-known mountains of the Americas, men of the United States Geodetic Survey measure and map the earth.

However, not all those who risk their lives and endure the hardships of struggling to rugged heights do it as part of their work. The men and women who climb mountains give different reasons for trying to reach altitudes never attained before. Some love the heights as other people love the vast sea or the wide prairies. Some do it for sport and recreation. Others want the sense of achievement that comes with accomplishing something difficult. Still others do it to realize a dream, held from childhood, to be higher than anything around them.

Whatever the reason they climb, most are not easily discouraged. They may suffer from frostbite or broken bones or lie helpless for days awaiting rescue, but when they are healed, they climb again.

Edward Whymper, one of the world's great climbers, reached the Matterhorn's summit at last on his eighth try. Other climbers made many attempts before they scaled such lofty summits as Aconcagua and Mount McKinley, highest peaks in the Western Hemisphere and in North America respectively.

But no matter how high the peak or how difficult the ascent, Mount Everest in the Himalayas, the world's highest mountain, was the real goal of most climbers. Ten different expeditions made the attempt, before the May morning in 1953 when two men, Edmond Hillary, a New Zealander, and Ten-

Tensing
Norkay

sing Norkay, a Nepalese, stood on the summit and looked out over the world.

REST AND RECREATION

Mountains demand hard work of those who make their living among them, but they also offer places for rest and recreation. In tropical lands people happily escape the heat by going to cooler altitudes for part of the year. Long ago it was mostly in summer that vacationers visited the mountains, but now winter sports

have made mountain resorts as crowded in winter as they are in the summer. Skiing is one of the popular sports that require slopes. The slopes of the Andes, as well as the Alps, are excellent for skiing, and the world's highest ski jump is in Bolivia, not far from La Paz. And more and more ski huts are dotting the mountains around the world.

Many people go to the mountains to re-gain their health. High up, where the air is pure, many sanatoria and hospitals have been built to treat special kinds of diseases.

The beauty of mountain scenery lures others. Thousands of people visit the mountains each year to enjoy waterfalls and rushing streams, cool green forests, and flowers and plants that grow only in the highlands.

As more people spend more time on the mountains they create work for those living there. Hotels and inns are opened to provide for the visitors. Guides are needed to take people on hunting trips and to lead climbing parties to the summits. Ski instructors find work there too.

Each year more people are sharing the mountains with the herders and miners and woodsmen. The rest of the world is discovering the remote villages, and is bringing in products and ideas from outside. Slowly mountain ways are changing. But in a world of rapid change, people still think of mountains as the everlasting hills.

Highest Mountain Peaks
of the Continents

PEAK	LOCATION	HEIGHT IN FEET
Everest	Asia	29,028
Aconcagua	South America	22,835
McKinley	North America	20,320
Kenya	Africa	17,040
Blanc	Europe	15,781
Markham	Antarctica	15,102
Kosciusko	Australia	7,352